# Petworth

*A souvenir guide*

West Sussex

**National Trust**

C000091012

# 'THE HOUSE OF ART'

*Everything solid, liberal, rich and English.*

The artist Benjamin Robert Haydon on Petworth in 1826

*The want of comforts, of regularity, and still more the total absence of cleanliness, made it, splendid and beautiful as it is, far from being agreeable …. People of all descriptions, without any connection or acquaintance with each other, are gathered together and huddled up at the dinner table.*

Henry Edward Fox on Petworth in 1828

That was how the painter John Constable described Petworth in the early 19th century. The house today still contains one of the best art collections in Britain – from dazzling portraits by Van Dyck to golden landscapes by Turner. But for all its austere façade and grand galleries, Petworth remains a family home, and there is much more to it than art.

## Another world

Connected to the house by an underground passage, the servants' quarters have survived almost intact. They give us a fascinating glimpse of all the various departments powering the complex machine that was a great country house and estate. Not only do the kitchens remain, but also, thanks to the huge Petworth archive, we can put names to the faces of the people who were photographed as they went about their daily work here.

## Park pleasures

On one side of the house lies the town of Petworth, which was never banished from view (as so often on country estates). On the other is the park – a magnificent landscape of grass, trees and water laid out in classic style by 'Capability' Brown and enhanced by the 3rd Earl of Egremont. Here you can still make out the views that Turner painted, or simply walk the dog, as the 3rd Earl loved to do.

## The makers of Petworth

*Above* Hieronymous Bosch's *Adoration of the Kings* hangs in the Somerset Room

*Opposite* Turner's *Petworth House from the Park... Dewy Morning*

The 10th Earl of Northumberland (1602–68), a friend and patron of Van Dyck, founded the Petworth picture collection in the 1630s. He attempted to steer a middle way during the Civil War, which earned him respect and suspicion.

The 6th Duke of Somerset (1662–1748) inherited Petworth by marrying Lady Elizabeth Percy, the heiress to the estate. In the 1680s he rebuilt the house much as you see it today, in a style that matched his nickname – 'the Proud Duke'.

The 2nd Earl of Egremont (1710–63) acquired many of the antique statues and huge Rococo mirrors in the house. He ate prodigiously, took no exercise and died suddenly.

The 3rd Earl of Egremont (1751–1837) was a shy man, but confident enough to disregard convention. A pioneer agriculturalist, philanthropist and race-horse owner, he is best known as a patron of British artists, in particular J. M. W. Turner.

# THE SOMERSET ROOM – *Landscapes large and small*

This room is named after the Proud Duke, who bought several of the pictures hung here. In the 1790s it was used as a servery, where food could be kept warm after its long journey from the Kitchen across the courtyard and before it was taken to table in the Square Dining Room. For this reason the 3rd Earl painted it white to match that room – a scheme renewed in 1995–6. Today, the room displays some of the masterpieces in the Petworth collection.

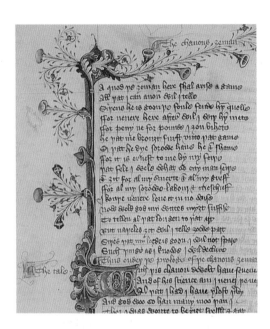

*Left* Claude's painting tells *the Old Testament story of Jacob and Laban*, but the figures are incidental to the main point of interest – the silvery Italian landscape. The picture was bought by the Proud Duke in 1686 and so was one of the first Claudes to reach Britain. It helped to start a fashion which inspired landscape gardens like Stourhead and Stowe with their lakes and classical temples. It also had a profound influence on the landscape paintings of Turner.

*Above left* The display case in the centre of the room contains an **illuminated manuscript** of Chaucer's *Canterbury Tales*. It was created by a single scribe in the 1420s, only 30 years after the Tales were written, making it one of the very earliest surviving texts of Chaucer's masterpiece. It may have been commissioned by the 2nd Earl of Northumberland, whose wife was Chaucer's great-niece.

*Above* Over the fireplace hangs Peter Lely's touching portrait of *the three younger children of Charles I*: from left to right, Henry (8 and still wearing a skirt, as young boys did at that time), Elizabeth (12) and James (14; later King James II). They were painted in 1647 at the height of the Civil War for the 10th Earl of Northumberland, who was keeping them under house arrest at Syon, his west London home, at the time. Shortly before his execution, Charles borrowed the painting to remind him of his children, whom he would never see again.

*Above* Over the mantelpiece is an exquisite little **group of Saints and Prophets**, painted on copper about 1605 by Adam Elsheimer. They probably once decorated a cabinet or altar belonging to a school or orphanage – hence the number of children depicted. The figures are immaculate, but the atmospheric detail in the background landscapes is truly astonishing – the equal of the vastly larger landscape by Claude which hangs nearby.

*Top and above* The Square
Dining Room is densely
hung with portraits and
a huge scene from
Shakespeare, much as it
was in Turner's day

*Right* Van Dyck's
posthumous portrait
of the Wizard Earl
(1564–1632) in his lavish
prison cell in the Tower
of London

# THE SQUARE DINING ROOM – *Restored to Turner's day*

The room was created about 1795 by the 3rd Earl, who hung it densely with pictures – like the rest of the house. Around 1827 Turner painted a watercolour of the far wall. The National Trust has used this to reconstruct the picture hang in the 3rd Earl's time, together with his choice of wall colour.

## Pictures

Dominating the far wall is Sir Joshua Reynolds's *Macbeth and the Witches*. Sadly, the picture is a darkened wreck, as Reynolds used unstable pigments. It was commissioned in 1786 by Alderman Boydell for his Shakespeare Gallery, a brave, but ultimately doomed, attempt to get British artists to give up lucrative portrait painting and try more elevated literary themes. Reynolds had to leave the picture unfinished in 1789, when he started to go blind. The little oval painting immediately above is a self-portrait by Reynolds.

Petworth is justly famous for its *group of portraits by Van Dyck*, the supreme delineator of the court of Charles I. The 10th Earl of Northumberland was one of Van Dyck's most generous patrons, commissioning the portrait of himself with his first wife Anne Cecil (who died shortly after it was painted) with their daughter Katherine.

The 10th Earl also got Van Dyck to paint a posthumous image of his father, the Wizard Earl, who is shown head-in-hand and surrounded by books in the attitude of a melancholy scholar. The Wizard Earl had much to be melancholy about, having been imprisoned for sixteen years in the Tower of London on suspicion of involvement in the Gunpowder Plot. But he spent his time productively, studying and conversing with some of the greatest minds of the age.

## Furniture

Between the windows are a matching *mirror* (or pier-glass) and side-table floridly carved in the Rococo style. After dark, candles were placed on the side-table, their power being doubled by the mirror behind. These pieces were among many supplied to the 2nd Earl in the 1760s by the London craftsmen James Whittle and Samuel Norman.

*Left* Van Dyck's portrait of his great patron, the 10th Earl of Northumberland, with the Countess and their daughter Katherine

**BANANA DRAMA**
The 2nd Lord Leconfield, who owned Petworth in the late 19th century, was told that home-grown bananas tasted quite different from the shop-bought variety. So he built a new hothouse specially to grow them. When the plant finally fruited, the banana was solemnly brought to table on a silver salver. He took one mouthful and promptly hurled the rest to the floor in disgust, declaring: 'Oh God, it tastes just like any other damn banana!'

# THE MARBLE HALL – *A proud entrance*

'The desolation of magnificence, an infinite vista of chambers, passages, and halls opening out of each other, apparently peopled only by human forms carved in marble.'

A VIEW OF PETWORTH IN THE 18TH CENTURY

The Proud Duke conceived this room as the main entrance to his new house, which it remained until the early 1870s, when the family built a more modest and less draughty entrance porch on the opposite side of the house.

The Proud Duke stamped his larger-than-life personality on this Dutch-style panelled hall: his coat of arms features prominently over the fireplaces, flanked by boldly carved representations of his heraldic supporters, the bull and the unicorn. Look out also for the Duke's arms engraved on the doorlocks. Just as in classical Roman villas, the niches were specifically designed for sculpture, much of which has been here since the Duke's day.

*Top* Somewhat surprisingly, in the 1860s the 1st Lord Leconfield used this room as a study, trying to make it a little more comfortable by introducing Victorian clutter: carpets, comfy chairs and even a billiard table

# THE BEAUTY ROOM – *Beauties and battlefields*

This room was also the work of the Proud Duke, who intended it as a tribute to Queen Anne and the leading ladies of her court, who appear in the portraits over the fireplace and in the upper register.

Originally, these portraits were full-length, but, declaring 'I do not want their petticoats', the 3rd Earl rolled up the lower part of each canvas so that he could create a shrine to the leading figures and events of the Napoleonic Wars in the space below. This includes a portrait of Napoleon, a bust of the Duke of Wellington and depictions of the battles of Vittoria and Waterloo, in which two of his sons had participated. In June 1814 the 3rd Earl had received the leaders of the alliance against Napoleon in the Marble Hall. A painting of the event hangs in the North Gallery.

*Above* Napoleon, painted by Thomas Phillips in 1802 during the brief period when he was not at war with Britain

*Above* The French Baroque
bust may be either of James
II or the man who
succeeded him, William III

*Right* The Grand Stairs.
The statue depicts Silenus
nursing the infant Bacchus

# THE GRAND STAIRS – *Murals with a message*

These stairs were designed to provide a suitably impressive link between the Proud Duke's state rooms on the ground floor and the bedrooms above.

The first version of this room was gutted by fire in 1714. When the Duke came to rebuild, he commissioned Louis Laguerre, the most celebrated mural painter of the time, to decorate the walls with a classical story that alludes to the earlier disaster: Prometheus stole fire from the gods, and man is punished by the opening of Pandora's box, which lets out all the world's evils (depicted on the ceiling). Immediately above the stairs, the Duchess of Somerset is shown riding in a triumphal chariot with her daughters. The murals were completed in 1720, a year before Laguerre's death, and their laborious baroque style was already starting to go out of fashion.

The ropes were first threaded through the balusters in the 1920s and were reinstated to prevent the present Lord Egremont's children falling through.

### Sculpture
The *marble bust* in the niche was sculpted by the French artist Honoré Pelle, who exploited the decorative potential of the curly wig to the full. It is either of James II or his overthrower, William III. Whoever the sitter, images like this show how influential French baroque taste was in Britain in the late 17th century.

### Carpet
The woollen carpet in the lower hall is another example of the influence of French taste, having been made in Exeter in 1758 in the style of the Savonnerie factory.

### Furniture
The shell-backed *walnut hall-chairs* are in the Italian sgabello style, with boards rather than legs. They were made about 1615–35, perhaps for the 9th or 10th Earls of Northumberland, both of whom travelled in Italy.

*Retrace your steps through the Beauty Room and Marble Hall to reach the Little Dining Room.*

## THE LITTLE DINING ROOM
*A servery for the Carved Room*

The panelling in this ante-room dates from the 1690s and includes the Proud Duke's coat of arms in the frieze. A watercolour by Turner shows a chamber orchestra playing here to entertain diners in the Carved Room next door.

### Pictures
The *portraits of beautiful young women* by Van Dyck are part of a group put together by the 10th Earl of Northumberland. There was a fashion for galleries of celebrity beauties across Europe, which also inspired the portraits in the Beauty Room. The *fragments of St James and a donor* are attributed to one of the greatest of early Flemish artists, Rogier van der Weyden.

*Top* The 17th-century walnut hall-chairs are Italian in style

*Above* The Little Dining Room

# THE CARVED ROOM – *Art, nature and history*

AN EVENING MEAL IN THE
CARVED ROOM IN 1828
*'The dinner was of the first
order, turtle, venison, moor
game, &c. without stint. The
servants, too, very numerous
tho' most of them very
advanced in years and
tottered, and comical in their
looks. The wax candles were
sufficiently numerous to
light us up well tho' we were
at one end of a room sixty
feet long, the wainscot of
which was Gibbons' carving
in wood.'*

About 1690 the Proud Duke created a room to show off Grinling Gibbons's carvings, which prominently feature his ducal coronet, star of the Order of the Garter and classical vases (alluding to his learning and generosity as a patron). The room was, however, originally only half its present size. It was not until the 1780s that the 3rd Earl took down a wall in the centre to make the long room we see today. He considerably rearranged the carvings and added more in the same style commissioned from the 19th-century carver Jonathan Ritson.

In the late 1820s the 3rd Earl had the brilliant idea of installing four landscapes by Turner within Gibbons-style carvings below the historic full-length portraits. He got the artist to produce full-size compositional sketches so that he could judge the effect before proceeding with the commission, which included two views of Petworth. The Turners may seem uncomfortably low to a standing visitor. But you should remember that the 3rd Earl used the Carved Room primarily for dining. When seated, his dinner guests could look easily from Turner's golden visions of Petworth park out through the windows to the park itself. This rare melding of art and nature was reinstated by the National Trust in 2000–2.

*Right* The Carved Room cleverly combines Turner landscapes, historic portraits and carvings by Grinling Gibbons

### Carve his name with pride

Grinling Gibbons means wood-carving to most people. He transformed blocks of limewood into miraculously realistic representations of delicate fur, feathers or flower petals, arranged in decorative garlands. His achievements inspired contemporary imitators like John Selden, who lived locally and was responsible for some of the carvings here. Selden is thought to have died saving Gibbons's work from the 1714 fire.

### Pictures

In the centre of the near wall is a full-length portrait of Charles I's queen, *Henrietta Maria, with her favourite dwarf, Jeffrey Hudson.* She first encountered Hudson when, aged seven and still only 46cm high, he leapt out of a pie at a party. During the Civil War he fled with the Queen to France, where he killed a man in a duel and was expelled from her court.

Left of the fireplace are matching portraits of *the 6th Duke and Duchess of Somerset,* who made this room. Many stories testify to the Duke's arrogance. When one of his daughters dared to sit down in his presence (he was asleep at the time), he docked £20,000 from her inheritance. But on the other hand he loved music and poetry and was an enlightened patron; his stiffness may also be partly explained by his stammer.

'The most superb monument of his skill.'

HORACE WALPOLE ON GRINLING GIBBONS'S WORK AT PETWORTH

*Above* Henry VIII in the classic pose invented by Holbein. Henry was 46 at the time, but looks younger, and his widely planted legs have been artificially elongated to make him appear even more swaggeringly impressive

*Left* Wood-carvings by Grinling Gibbons

*Top* The Red Room

*Above* The Leconfield Aphrodite; a classical Greek bust attributed to Praxiteles

*Right A peasant family* by the Le Nain brothers

# THE RED ROOM – *Portraits of rich and poor*

Red has always been a popular colour on which to hang Old Master pictures. This scheme was devised by the 3rd Earl in 1806 and restored in 2002 by the National Trust, which also reinstated the picture hang recorded in a watercolour by Turner.

### Pictures

Either side of the door to the North Gallery are *Van Dyck's portraits of Sir Robert Shirley and his wife Teresia Khan*. They were probably painted in 1622 in Rome, where Sir Robert was serving as the Shah of Persia's ambassador to the Pope. Van Dyck does splendid justice to the Shirleys' gorgeous eastern clothes: Sir Robert wears a cloak of cloth of gold embroidered with oriental figures, while Lady Shirley sits by a tent in a jewelled headdress with her pet monkey.

To the right of the far door hangs the Le Nain brothers' *A peasant family* of 1642. The Le Nains specialised in calm, dignified, but direct depictions of the poor like this.

### Sculpture

The so-called *Leconfield Aphrodite* is the most famous piece of ancient sculpture in the house. It came from a 4th-century BC full-length figure of the Greek goddess of love attributed to the Athenian sculptor Praxiteles. Like many classical sculptures, it has had its nose repaired, probably in the 18th century by Bartolommeo Cavaceppi, a famous restorer-dealer of the period.

### Furniture

The *commode* is by the greatest French furniture maker of the early 18th century, André-Charles Boulle, who gave his name to a style of complex cut-out brass inlay. Look closely at the gilt-brass (ormolu) corner mounts, which are superbly detailed.

**PETWORTH AT WAR**

During the Second World War, Petworth served as headquarters of Commando Group. The ground floor was stripped of pictures and sculpture, and the large bare rooms were partitioned. The CO used part of the Red Room as his office. Children from the Chelsea Day Nursery slept in the servants' block, and Canadian troops camped in the park. One inhabitant remembers life as rather quiet, allowing time for amateur theatricals.

*Left* Lady Shirley, painted by Van Dyck in colourful eastern silks

# THE NORTH GALLERY – *An art gallery in a country house*

The North Gallery is a rare surviving example of a purpose-built art gallery from the early 19th century, when British collectors dominated Europe.

**A BAFFLED VISITOR IN 1828**
'It is in vain to attempt anything like a detailed description of the immensity of pictures on the ground floor of the house .... Then they are all mixed up together, good and bad, ... and he [the 3rd Earl] is perpetually changing their places.'

*Above* William Blake's *Last Judgement*

*Opposite* The South Corridor is filled mainly with antique sculpture collected by the 2nd Earl of Egremont in the mid-18th century

The gallery grew in three stages in a vain attempt to provide enough space for the family's burgeoning art collections. In 1754–64 the 2nd Earl turned an external cloister into the South Corridor to display some of his antique statuary. In 1824–5 the 3rd Earl added the Central Corridor and, shortly afterwards, the North Bay. All three spaces are top-lit to offer the best conditions to view the works of art. The 3rd Earl tinkered with the skylights until he had got them exactly right. Oil lamps and then gas lights allowed for night-time viewing.

Turner's watercolours show that the walls were painted white – the colour favoured for showing contemporary art today. But in the 3rd Earl's day, much of the art here was contemporary. The walls were only painted their present dark red tone in 1873.

## Sculpture

Following his Grand Tour of Italy in 1729–30, the 2nd Earl assembled a superb collection of *antique statues and busts*, most of which are crowded in the South Corridor in niches and on pedestals and wall brackets. Many have had missing pieces replaced, as was the fashion in the 18th century.

The 3rd Earl deliberately mixed his purchases of *modern sculpture* with his father's classical pieces, because he believed they were just as good, and so that the contemporary sculptors he patronised could learn from ancient examples.

Dominating the North Bay is *St Michael*

*subduing Satan*, 1826, by the leading Neo-classical sculptor John Flaxman, who took the pose from a painting by Raphael in the Louvre. It was carved from a single block of marble (apart from the spear). The 3rd Earl had suggested the subject and, according to the inscription on the base, believed that Flaxman's statue 'was hardly surpassed by the most celebrated productions of ancient times, and certainly by none of his own'. The rest of the North Bay is given over to statues and busts by the Irish sculptor John Carew, including, on the left, *Venus, Vulcan and Cupid*, and, on the right, *Prometheus and Pandora*. The 3rd Earl bought so much of Carew's work that he predicted, 'When I am gone, he will be a beggar' – correctly, as it turned out.

## Pictures

The North Gallery reveals the breadth and generosity of the 3rd Earl's tastes as a collector of contemporary painting. Turner is well represented, not just by views of land and sea (*The Egremont Seapiece*), but also by Shakespearean subjects such as *Jessica*, which has always been controversial: one early critic described her as 'emerging from a pot of mustard'. But there is also much by Turner's now less well-known contemporaries: portraits by Thomas Phillips, literary subjects by C. R. Leslie and William Hilton; and history paintings by James Northcote. The William Blake watercolours were probably commissioned by the 3rd Earl's wife Elizabeth.

## THE CHAPEL – *A theatre of worship*

The Chapel was probably built in the early 1300s and is the best preserved interior from the medieval Petworth of the Percys. In the late 17th century the Proud Duke transformed it with a grand Baroque flourish.

The Proud Duke commissioned the **plasterwork ceiling** and the **woodwork**, including the carved curtain, which rises to reveal the family pew like the royal box in an Italian opera house. To complete the theatrical effect, angels carry aloft the Duke's coat of arms and coronet. The angels are probably based on the very similar figures carved by Grinling Gibbons for the Queen's Chapel in St James's Palace in 1682.

Don't miss the delicately carved **cherubs' heads** that top the choir stalls: no two are the same, and all are filled with boisterous life. The heraldic **stained glass**, which was made about 1600, records the marriages of the Percy family.

Directly above the Chapel is the Old Library, which artists, including Turner, used as a studio, when they were staying at Petworth.

## THE SERVANTS' QUARTERS – *A production line*

Built in the mid-18th century, the Servants' Quarters are little changed from Victorian times and are shown today as they looked between 1920 and 1940. Designed as an efficient production line, food and other raw materials were delivered to the back door, then stored and processed in larders, dairies and other rooms until finally being prepared in the kitchens. At the opposite end, the business of the estate was conducted in the estate offices and the first floor provided bedrooms for the indoor staff – with separate staircases for the male and female staff at opposite ends of the corridor.

### The servants

Running Petworth House demanded skill and expertise and a large army of staff.

A very strict hierarchy prevailed with the house steward and later the butler in charge of around 38 indoor staff. The housekeeper supervised the female staff and the chef the kitchen staff. The other upper servants were the lady's maid, the valet and any governesses and they enjoyed their own separate sitting rooms and dining room where they were waited on by more junior staff. As well as the staff working in the house, there were 24 grooms and coachmen and 25 gardeners, plus many more on the wider estate.

*Above* The Chapel

*Opposite* The indoor servants in the 1880s

THE ESTATE OFFICES
These recently restored offices were built in 1803–5 for the 3rd Earl's go-ahead new agent, William Tyler, who managed the Egremonts' southern estates. There were also separate, vast land holdings in Cumberland, which together brought in over £100,000 a year. The building was carefully sited near the 3rd Earl's private quarters, but away from the Kitchen and the risk of fire. Barred windows kept it secure, as large amounts of cash would be collected here on rent days. Over almost a millennia, the estate has generated a huge archive, which can now be consulted at the West Sussex Record Office in Chichester thanks to the generosity of Lord Egremont.

*Right* The Kitchen

*Opposite* Ice-creams in the Larder

### The Tunnel
Food, linen, coal and other necessities were carried across to the house by the footmen, housemaids and 'odd men' through an underground tunnel. This kept the noise and smells of cooking as well as the risk of fire well away from the family's own rooms.

### The Kitchens
In the main kitchen, cooking styles spanning 300 years can be seen from the traditional open-fire roasting range, to the Victorian steam ovens and the solid fuel cooker and electric ovens.

The chef was assisted sometimes by a pastry chef and a roasting chef as well as kitchen maids and a scullery man. The kitchens produced on average 100 meals a day and sometimes three or four times that number.

### The Pastry
Away from the heat of the main kitchen, the Pastry was ideal for making pies, biscuits, cakes and pastries. The old pastry oven can be seen in the adjoining lobby.

### The Scullery
The magnificent boiler produced steam for the kitchen equipment and for the circular copper to heat the water. Food was cleaned and prepared in here and pots and pans washed.

### The Chef's Sitting Room
The Chef was the most highly paid member of staff along with the butler. In this room he would plan his menus, scrutinise accounts and store expensive or unusual items.

### The Larder
A general-purpose storage and preparation room supplemented by a separate meat larder and winter dairy.

### The Still Room
Jams, marmalades and pickles were made here as well as the early morning and afternoon tea trays, soft drinks and fruit juices.

# THE PARK AND PLEASURE GROUNDS

## C. R. Leslie watches Turner sailing paper boats on the lake

'He rigged scraps of paper torn from his sketch book, upon three little sticks stuck in a bit of board to represent a full-rigged ship, which to my great delight he then launched upon the lake.'

### The Park

'Capability' Brown transformed the settings of scores of country houses with his 'natural' style of landscape gardening. But Petworth is perhaps the supreme surviving example, despite the damage caused to the trees by the 1987 Great Storm. In 1751 Brown laid out the vast expanse of grass that rolls gently down from the west front to the serpentine lake, which is the focus of the composition. Framing all this are seemingly natural clumps of trees. Deer still nibble the grass. This is the landscape loved by Turner and by the 3rd Earl, who added the vases and other statuary that dot the park, and did much of the present planting.

### The Pleasure Grounds

The Pleasure Grounds lie on the rising ground to the north of the house. This is a woodland garden divided by meandering walks and open glades, the whole enclosed by a ha-ha (concealed ditch). 'Capability' Brown suggested adding the Doric temple and Ionic rotunda as focal points amid the trees.

Spring brings carpets of primroses, followed by daffodils, bluebells and fritillaries. The trees in the Pleasure Grounds suffered particularly badly in the Great Storm, and will take many years to recover, despite much replanting and excellent growing conditions. But an unusually wide range of trees and shrubs still flourish, from crab apples and Spanish chestnut to American oaks, rhododendrons and tulip trees.

*Left* The garden staff in the 1880s

*Below* This painting by W. F. Witherington records the fête organised by the 3rd Earl in May 1835 for 4,000 people

*Opposite* The rotunda in spring

HONI SOIT QVI MAL Y PENSE